www.bobhartley.org

CONTENTS

Page 4-6	Introduction to the Hope Hearing Journal
Page 7-20	Hope in God Questions
8-13	About Your Relationship with Him
14-20	About a Situation in your Life
Page 21-42	Hope in People Questions
21-27	About a Friend or Loved One
28-42	"14 Questions" to Ask About Another Person
Page 43-50	Hope in the Next Generation Questions
Page 51-54	Hope in Prayer Questions
Page 55-60	Hope in Cities and Nations Questions
Page 61-70	Additional Hope Resources
62	Hopeless to Hope Chart
63	Hope Scriptures
64-67	Frequently Used Hartley Institute Terms
68	Hope Tools
69	Hope is…

INTRODUCTION TO THE HOPE HEARING JOURNAL

Vision of Cities and Nations that will Love God Well and Hope in Him

In 1983, Bob asked the Lord over and over again, "God what is on your heart?" God showed him that He is Bringing forth radiant Hope-filled Cities and nations, families, businesses, organizations and every arena that will love Him well and hope in Him.

So what does that look like? What does it look like to move from despair to hope in your spheres of relationship? HOPE is confident expectation in the goodness of God in all of life... not just in eternity but TODAY!

God is initiating a change in the NATURE of Christianity from despair, doubt, and fear being a normal accepted reality in the life of a believer, to an understanding that our inheritance is righteousness peace and joy in the Holy Spirit, and we are to be full of hope in our daily lives and spheres of influence. How does this happen?

A new understanding of who God is, and who we are in Him:
God is "FOR US," He is the God of ALL of Life, and He desires every Person to have a Multi-Colored Coat- Micah 4:4- "own vine and fig tree"

Building Hope Centers

As a result of this new understanding, Hope Centers are coming forth across the earth in every area of society. A Hope Center is more than just a physical location. It is a decision to live and build out hope wherever we live and function. A Hope Center is anywhere that a Hope or a God view is moved into the CENTER & where His presence is the answer to all situations and circumstances.

Here are some different types of Hope Centers:
- *Church/Ministry Hope Centers*
- *Kingdom/ Business Hope Centers*
- *Education Hope Centers*
- *Arts & Entertainment/ Media Hope Centers*
- *Family Hope Centers*
- *Community or National Hope Centers*
- *Individuals as Hope Centers*

The Process and Royal Journey to Get There

The Lord began to show me a holy progression into His presence called the Journey of Hope. He was calling 50 million "Hope Bringers" to walk out this biblical journey like Song of Solomon 1-8. This reveals how we are to build a life of Hope in God in every area and every season of life. He showed me that this journey is all about discovering the God of Hope in deeper ways and growing in intimacy with Him. It is about thriving in this life, not just surviving until He returns! He came to give us life and He brings us life more abundant and it's available today!

The Golden Keys of Adoration & Asking

Many years ago, I began the first step on this journey, which is the Hope Room, or the Adoration Room experience where Face to Face Prayer happens. I discovered that this journey is not a method or program, but meeting with the one you love. It's all about relationship with the man Christ Jesus. I found that adoration prayer is the first and "always" step on the journey, it is the only thing that matters!
- *Psalm 34:3—"O magnify the Lord with me, and let us exalt His name together."*
- *Psalm 100:1,4-5—"Shout joyfully to the Lord, all the earth. Serve the Lord with gladness; come before Him with joyful singing. Enter His gates with thanksgiving and His courts with praise. Give thanks to Him, bless His name. For the Lord is good; His loving-kindness is everlasting and His faithfulness to all generations."*

The Importance of Asking and Inquiring of His Hopeful Heart

Questions are really an onramp, a navigational tool into the deeper waters of His heart. Understanding His nature and who He is and His purpose for us. God is inviting us into that place of deep friendship and relationship with him where we not only get answers but something more important than answers.

So, Why Ask Questions?

There are several reasons why questions are important. First of all, we are invited. The bible speaks over and over of our asking. Isaiah 1 and 18 is an invitation for the Counsel table of the Lord, where we sit and reason with Him. We come into agreement with His purpose and direction.

So, Why Ask Questions?

The second reason is because He has the answers. This may seem obvious but most people, including me spend time in the "figure it out" room. At the counsel table of the Lord, God has already figured it out and it's good. He's waiting there to give us perspective, insight and understanding that changes our life.

The third reason is because He offers something that is more important than answers. Often we're looking for the black and white of the situation. The answers, the way through. The process of the counsel table of the Lord is not a fortune cookie, an ATM, a question and answer site where you put in the question and an answer pops out like a gumball machine. God offers so much more than that. He offers intimacy, deep friendship, perspective, an eternal relationship that grows deep and nurtures over time. He offers the true secrets of His heart.

The fourth reason is because we gain a new view. Miracles of hope are born for Miracles of perspective. As we begin to ask questions concerning every area of our life, we gain His perspective, God's view, a love view, and a hopeful view in life and it changes everything.

Conclusion

There's an experience and breakthrough in hope that comes as we ask questions and God gives us the questions to ask Him. If we cooperate in that process, a deep dialogue begins to happen. It opens deep areas in our hearts that we're not even aware of. It allows God to grow us, build us and bring us along in a way that is ultimately for our higher good and benefit!

How to Use the Hope Hearing Journal

This journal contains hope-filled questions that have been given by the Lord to accelerate our hearts into deep communion and dialogue with Him in all of life.

Before you begin, take time to posture your heart in adoration, adoring and magnifying who He is, in the place of thanksgiving and praise. If you do not have an *Adoration Prayer Book*, visit bobhartley.org and get yours today!

Now begin to ask Him these hope-filled questions and prepare your heart for a new journey into the knowledge of who He is at the Counsel Table of the Lord. You have a seat of honor at His table! Enjoy the journey with Him!
- *Psalm 27:4- "One thing I have desired of the LORD, that will I seek: that I may dwell in the house of the LORD all the days of my life, to behold the beauty of the LORD, and to inquire in His temple."*

Hope in God Questions

"Hope in God" Questions" help to move us from hopelessness in God to an unshakable hope in who He is, Hope in God is a redeemed view of Him in all of life. It is choosing to believe the truth of who God is, that He's bigger and better than any circumstance or situation, and He is "for us." Hope in God is a healed and expanded view of God in all of life that helps us to see that....

- God is enough for every circumstance
- His presence is the answer
- His friendship is our ultimate reward

"You are the most excellent of men and your lips have been anointed with grace, since God has blessed you forever." Psalm 45:2

HOPE IN GOD QUESTIONS
...about **Your Relationship** with Him

God says to you...

"Ask Me what you mean to Me and My heart."

HOPE IN GOD QUESTIONS
...about **Your Relationship** with Him

God says to you...

"Ask Me what is the long term plan for success of Our relationship for the next 30 years."

HOPE IN GOD QUESTIONS
...about **Your Relationship** with Him

God says to you...

"Ask Me if I will help you have more than a casual relationship with Me."

HOPE IN GOD QUESTIONS
...about **Your Relationship** with Him

God says to you...

"Ask Me why you mean everything to me."

HOPE IN GOD QUESTIONS
...about **Your Relationship** with Him

God says to you...

"Ask Me who I could be to you in all situations."

HOPE IN GOD QUESTIONS
...about **Your Relationship** with Him

God says to you...

"Ask Me what I like about you holding Me."

HOPE IN GOD QUESTIONS
...about a **Situation** in Your Life

God says to you...

""Ask, Me what part of My nature I am revealing to you in this situation."

HOPE IN GOD QUESTIONS
...about a **Situation** in Your Life

God says to you...

"Ask Me how much I have abundance of life and hope for you in this situation."

HOPE IN GOD QUESTIONS
...about a **Situation** in Your Life

God says to you...

"Ask Me if I am more than enough for you in this situation."

HOPE IN GOD QUESTIONS
... about a **Situation** in Your Life

God says to you...

"Ask Me about the hope miracles I want to provide for you in this situation."

HOPE IN GOD QUESTIONS
... about a **Situation** in Your Life

God says to you...

"Ask Me if there is anything too difficult for Me."

HOPE IN GOD QUESTIONS
... about a **Situation** in Your Life

God says to you...

"Ask Me about the hope miracles I want to provide for you in this situation."

_____
_____
_____
_____
_____
_____
_____
_____
_____
_____
_____
_____
_____
_____
_____
_____
_____
_____
_____
_____
_____
_____
_____
_____

Hope in People Questions

"Hope in People" Questions" help to move us from hopelessness in people to an unshakable hope in who God is in others   Hope in People is a redeemed view of people that sees them through the eyes of Jesus and then calls forth the unique value in each one, focusing on who they were created to be versus what they are not,. Hope in People is agreement with the heart of God for others that helps us to see that…

- People matter (every single one)
- We need to make room in our hearts for others (because God has)
- Love is worth it (even when it's not easy)

"I praise you because I am fearfully and wonderfully made; your works are wonderful, I know that full well."   **Psalm 139:14**

HOPE IN PEOPLE QUESTIONS
...about a **Friend** or **Loved One**

God says to you...

"Ask Me for a Life Scripture that unlocks _____'s heart and unlocks their love for Me."

HOPE IN PEOPLE QUESTIONS
... about a **Friend** or **Loved One**

God says to you...

"Ask Me who _____ is to Me."

HOPE IN PEOPLE QUESTIONS
... about a **Friend** or **Loved One**

God says to you...

"Ask Me to tell you about _____'s past / present / future from My hope filled eyes."

HOPE IN PEOPLE QUESTIONS
...about a **Friend** or **Loved One**

God says to you...

"Ask Me for a Life Scripture that unlocks Charles 's heart and unlocks their love for Me."

HOPE IN PEOPLE QUESTIONS
...about a **Friend** or **Loved One**

God says to you....

"Ask Me if _____ *has all they need to succeed and soar."*

HOPE IN PEOPLE QUESTIONS
...about a **Friend** or **Loved One**

God says to you...

"Ask Me about _____*'s special unique inheritance in Me."*

HOPE IN PEOPLE QUESTIONS
"14 Questions" to Ask God about another Person

God says to you...

1. "Ask Me for the special hope filled song or poem I have written for them over their lives."

HOPE IN PEOPLE QUESTIONS
"14 Questions" to Ask God about another Person

God says to you...

2. *"Ask Me to tell you about their past / present / future from My hope filled eyes."*

HOPE IN PEOPLE QUESTIONS
"14 Questions" to Ask God about another Person

God says to you...

"Ask Me for a "Wonderful Enlightening Story" or hopeful picture for them."

HOPE IN PEOPLE QUESTIONS
"14 Questions" to Ask God about another Person

God says to you...

4. *"Ask Me for a Life Scripture that unlocks their heart and unlocks love for Me."*

HOPE IN PEOPLE QUESTIONS
"14 Questions" to Ask God about another Person

God says to you...

5. *"Ask Me what state are they in (3 Ws) & what Face of Me they need to encounter in this season of their lives."*
   - *Wounded - God as Healer*
   - *Why - God as Guide*
   - *Willing - God as the Builder*

HOPE IN PEOPLE QUESTIONS
"14 Questions" to Ask God about another Person

God says to you...

6. *"Ask Me about past prophetic words or hope filled promises of My heart that confirm their identity in Me."*

HOPE IN PEOPLE QUESTIONS
"14 Questions" to Ask God about another Person

God says to you...

7. "Ask Me about their personal inheritance in hope in Me."

HOPE IN PEOPLE QUESTIONS
"14 Questions" to Ask God about another Person

God says to you...

8. *"Ask Me which Nine Spiritual gifts from I Corinthians 12 I have given them."*
   - *Wisdom*
   - *Word of knowledge*
   - *Faith*
   - *Healing*
   - *Miracles*
   - *Prophecy*
   - *Discernment of spirits*
   - *Various kinds of tongues*
   - *Interpretation of tongues*

HOPE IN PEOPLE QUESTIONS
"14 Questions" to Ask God about another Person

God says to you...

9. *"Ask Me which of the 5-fold ministries from Ephesians 4 I have called them to."*

HOPE IN PEOPLE QUESTIONS
"14 Questions" to Ask God about another Person

God says to you...

10. Ask Me which of the Eight Motivational gifts from Romans 12:6-8 I have given them."
- *Prophecy*
- *Ministry*
- *Teaching*
- *Exhortation*
- *Generosity*
- *Leadership*
- *Compassion*
- *Cheerfulness*

_____
_____
_____
_____
_____
_____
_____
_____
_____
_____
_____
_____
_____
_____
_____
_____
_____
_____

HOPE IN PEOPLE QUESTIONS
"14 Questions" to Ask God about another Person

God says to you...

11. *"Ask Me what different grains or temperaments they have."*
    - *Scattered cumin—artists need room & space*
    - *Wheat in rows—need structure*

HOPE IN PEOPLE QUESTIONS
"14 Questions" to Ask God about another Person

God says to you...

12. "Ask Me which of the ten Kingdom Callings they are called to."

- *Worship Army (Lydia)* - they change the atmosphere and bring the aroma of Christ into lives and situations.

- *Compassion Army (Boaz)* - called to make the city a place of praise, worship, joy, thanksgiving. Called to bring the 'incense' to the city.

- *Prayer and Presence Army (Daniel- hearers)* - weep over the city, long for the Lord to dwell, great lights in the midst of darkness, will bring the entrance of the Kingdom of God into every area of the city.

- *Oasis-Builders/Marketplace Redeemers - Culture Bringers (Abraham)* - have a marketplace calling and gifting, but loaded with ministry gifting as well.

- *Craftsmen (Bezalel)* - driven by the motive to craft for Him, to give Him the very best and have a revelation of the Creator God.

- *Treasure-Bringers (Cyrus's)* - line up to bring their best joyfully to Jesus, then run back as fast as they can to get more!

- *Cupbearers (Mordecai)* - prophetic influencers; in the right place at the right time with the right word. They are much bigger than their function.

- *Governors (Joseph)* - gifts of government: leadership and management. Their key is in the vision and the plan. Revelation of God the King revealed through them as they make the city a place of justice, order and peace.

- *City Builders (Joseph, Nehemiah)* - build a place for God to dwell, build cities of refuge and govern with wisdom, understanding and counsel.

- *Anointers (Samuel)* - Samuels will anoint kings. They equip marketplace apostles, prophets, evangelists, pastors and teachers; worship army, compassion army, prayer/presence army, etc.

_____

_____

_____

HOPE IN PEOPLE QUESTIONS
"14 Questions" to Ask God about another Person

God says to you...

13. *"Ask Me what they are to be Likened unto*
    - *Person - another biblical character (ex. Like David)*
    - *Plant - ex. Cedar, cypress etc*
    - *Animals - ex. Ishmael/donkey, Lion etc.*
    - *Object or Minerals - ex. Peter/Rock / David /A High Tower*

HOPE IN PEOPLE QUESTIONS
"14 Questions" to Ask God about another Person

God says to you...

14. Ask Me what season they are in (winter, spring, summer or fall) and why."

Hope in the Next Generation Questions

"Hope in the Next Generation" Questions" help to move us from hopelessness in the next generation to an unshakable hope in who God is in them This creates a desire to raise up youth in the true knowledge of the God of all of life and hope, and to really see them smile at their future. Hope in the next generation is a healed and expanded view of God in the next generation, which causes us to see that....

- The Next Generation is beautiful
- Their futures are worth fighting for
- They are a blessing

"He will restore the hearts of the fathers to their children and the hearts of the children to their fathers" Malachi 4:6

HOPE IN THE NEXT GENERATION QUESTIONS
...about **Young Ones** in your Life

God says to you...

"Ask Me what tools I want to give them to feed their hearts."

HOPE IN THE NEXT GENERATION QUESTIONS
... about **Young Ones** in your Life

God says to you...

"Ask Me if I am enough to change this generation."

HOPE IN THE NEXT GENERATION QUESTIONS
...about **Young Ones** in your Life

God says to you...

"Ask Me what kind of future they have in Me."

HOPE IN THE NEXT GENERATION QUESTIONS
... about **Young Ones** in your Life

God says to you...

"Ask Me what I have named the next generation. They are not Generation X...Y... or Z, I have named them Generation Hope."

HOPE IN THE NEXT GENERATION QUESTIONS
...about **Young Ones** in your Life

God says to you...

"Ask Me about their unique part, their extraordinary gift, and the unfolding of their history in this time."

HOPE IN THE NEXT GENERATION QUESTIONS
... about **Young Ones** in your Life

God says to you...

"*Ask Me how to celebrate them and see them the way the bible says they are a blessing and reward, and how they are more than able to survive and thrive in the hour we are in.*"

Hope in Prayer Questions

"Hope in Prayer" Questions" help to move us to a redeemed view of prayer that re-establishes the principal of 'building on our knees' in devotional and intercessory prayer as our 'Chief Building Methodology'. It is being committed to knowing God in all of life; to stop and be with Him first before building, to consider God and His plan first and foremost. Hope in prayer is a healed and expanded view of prayer that helps us to see that....

- All things are possible through prayer
- Prayer is necessary
- Prayer changes everything

"For Zion's sake I will not keep silent..."
Isaiah 62:1

HOPE IN PRAYER QUESTIONS
...about Dialoguing with God

God says to you...

"Ask Me how prayer works."

HOPE IN PRAYER QUESTIONS
...about Dialoguing with God

God says to you...

"Ask Me what prayer means to Me and My heart."

Hope in Cities & Nations Questions

"Hope in Cities and Nations" Questions" help to move us to a redeemed view of how God views cities and nations that gives us confidence that God loves cities and nations and has great plans and a future for them. God has the ability and desire to change a nation in a day. Hope in cities and nations helps us to see that...

- Loving your city and nation is loving God well, for He loves cities and nations
- His desire is for us to truly dwell in our cities and take ownership
- We are called to be the ones who bring transformation

"Then they will rebuild the ancient ruins, ... they will repair the ruined cities...."
Isaiah 61:4

HOPE IN CITIES AND NATIONS QUESTIONS
... about **your Community and Nation**

God says to you...

"Ask Me why I chose this city."

HOPE IN CITIES AND NATIONS QUESTIONS
... about **your Community and Nation**

God says to you...

"Ask Me if I believe in this city enough for it to be transformed."

HOPE IN CITIES AND NATIONS QUESTIONS
... about **your Community and Nation**

God says to you...

""Ask Me for My plan for Hope Centers in your city and nation."

HOPE IN CITIES AND NATIONS QUESTIONS
... about **your Community and Nation**

God says to you...

"Ask Me for My 100-year growth plan of hope for your city and nation."

Additional Hope Resources

HOPELESS TO ⟶ HOPE!

Focused on the problem	Focused on a favorable future
Apathetic	Appreciates life
Pessimistic	Optimistic
Produces skepticism with doubts	Builds faith with expectations
Strives for existence	Works hard
Inactive or merely busy	Productive
Enslaved	Free
Sad and angry	Joy and laughter
Expects a handout	Offers a handout
Victim	Over comer
Draining	Life-giving
Dependent	Responsible
Tears others down	Builds others up
Illness	Health
Financial dependence	Financial sufficiency and content
Survive in a holding pattern	Advance the Kingdom of God
Are the problem	Solve the problem
Desiring "wants"	Content with met "needs"
Delusions	Sound reasoning
Frustrated and empty	Fulfilled
Recipient of curses	Recipient of blessings
Demonic harassment	Angelic assistance
Disobedient to God	Obedient to God
Skeptical of God's character	Believe God's promises
Distrust authority	Trust authority
Burdensome	Humorous
Sees darkness	Sees light
Sees nothing good	Sees potential
Remorseful about sin	Repentant for sin
Harbors unforgiveness	Forgives readily
Defeated	Victorious
Negative influence	Positive influence
Bitter	Grateful

An individual with Hope makes a positive contribution. They know who God is and who they are in God.

HOPE SCRIPTURES

- *Psalm 25:3* - "No one whose hope is in you will ever be put to shame, but they will be put to shame who are treacherous without excuse."

- *Psalm 25:5* - "guide me in your truth and teach me, for you are God my Savior, and my hope is in you all day long."

- *Psalm 33:22* - "May your unfailing love rest upon us, O LORD, even as we put our hope in you."

- *Psalm 130:7* - "O Israel, put your hope in the LORD, for with the LORD is unfailing love and with him is full redemption.'

- *Psalm 146:5* - "Blessed is he whose help is the God of Jacob, whose hope is in the LORD his God,"

- *Proverbs 23:18* - "There is surely a future hope for you, and your hope will not be cut off."

- *Isaiah 40:31* - "but those who hope in the LORD will renew their strength. They will soar on wings like eagles; they will run and not grow weary, they will walk and not be faint."

- *Hosea 2:15* - "There I will give her back her vineyards, and will make the Valley of Achor a door of hope. There she will sing as in the days of her youth, as in the day she came up out of Egypt."

- *Micah 7:7* - "But as for me, I watch in hope for the LORD, I wait for God my Savior; my God will hear me."

- *Matthew 12:21* - "In his name the nations will put their hope."

- *Romans 4:18* - "Against all hope, Abraham in hope believed and so became the father of many nations, just as it had been said to him, "So shall your offspring be."

- *John 10:10* — "The thief comes only to steal and kill and destroy; I came that they may have life, and have it abundantly."

- *Mark 10:29-30* - "there is no one who has left house or brothers or sisters or mother or father or children or farms, for My sake and for the gospel's sake, ³⁰but that he will receive a hundred times as much now in the present age..."

FREQUENTLY USED **HARTLEY INSTITUTE TERMS**

HOPE REFORMATION TERMS

HOPE: is "an anticipation & belief in God for good in all of life and the future that changes everything."
- HOPE enables us to see a very, very, very long way out in confidence in Him!
- HOPE enables us to see another future.
- HOPE IS A "perspective OF ABUNDANT LIFE."
- HOPE IS AN "Unseen invisible power."
- Love SECURES a heart, but HOPE ADVANCES a heart.
- First love is sweet, second love is deep, but third love is a FORCE CALLED HOPE.
- Romans 15:13- May the God of hope fill you with all joy and peace as you trust in him...

HOPE REFORMATION: A movement of God in the earth at this time, where not only the ex-pression of Christianity has changed to a "sermon on the mount" lifestyle but where the nature of Christianity is changing to express the very nature of God as the God of Hope. Through the first reformation we learned that we are saved through grace only, not by works, giving us eternal security and answering the question: "how are we saved?" The Hope Reformation answers the question, "how then shall we live?" It opens up the door to walk with God and commune with Him and bring His presence into all of life.
- Exodus 33:15- if Your presence does not go with us, do not send us from this place.
- Hosea 2:15- He turns the Valley of Achor (challenge) into a door of hope.

HOPE REFORMERS: those with a 3rd perspective, not that of the world or their own, but God's perspective of hope- a view from God that transforms hopelessness and despair to a life filled with hope- they restore hope in God in all arenas of life and in the 5 Pillars of Hope.
- Psalm 34:5- Those who look to him are radiant; their faces are never covered with shame.

HOPE CENTERS: a Hope Center is more than just a physical location. It is a decision to live out and build out hope wherever we live and function. A Hope Center is anywhere that a Hope or a God view is moved into the CENTER & where His presence is the answer to all situations and circumstances. Hebrews 3:13.

MARKETPLACE REFORMERS: Marketplace Reformers are ones who are anchored in the knowledge of God and bring hope into the marketplace. They provide an OASIS Hope Centers – rich veins in these times and seasons. They have a unique Knowledge of God's voice and they perceive the "Unique Value" and "Knowledge of God" to be discovered in the marketplace. Marketplace Reformers open up the gates of cites and nations (as in Psalm 24) and invite the King of glory in to all of life.

FREQUENTLY USED **HARTLEY INSTITUTE TERMS**

ACTS PRAYER MODEL

ADORATION PRAYER: Adoring and magnifying God, face to face, expressing love and appreciation and a thankful heart, primarily for who He is. It's not about asking, it's about falling in love with Him as we see Him for who He really is. Adoration unlocks the knowledge of who God is.

Key scriptures for adoration in Business and Life
- Psalm 44:4 – saved by the light of His presence!
- Micah 4 – magnify Him above all else!

CONFESSION PRAYER: As we focus on Him in adoration, we realize our great need for Him, and begin to confess the Colossians 1:27 reality of Christ in us the hope of Glory. We have four main areas that we confess God in and through: ourselves, other people, circumstances and promises through all the day. Confession prayer is agreeing with what God says and declaring it in our day to day walk with Him with so much power.

Key scriptures for Confession
- 2 Cor 5:17- "Therefore if anyone is in Christ, {he is} a new creature; the old things passed away; behold, new things have come."

THANKSGIVING PRAYER: the act of giving thanks and grateful acknowledgement of the benefits and favor of God in our lives. We are always to give thanks at the table of the Lord (Malachi 1). Our gratitude is an attitude. Throughout scripture, we see that it is good to give thanks We come before His presence with thanksgiving and His courts with praise

Key scriptures for Thanksgiving
- 1 Chronicles 16:7- That day David first committed .. this psalm of thanks to the LORD
- Psalm 26:7- proclaiming aloud your praise and telling of all your wonderful deeds.

SUPPLICATION PRAYER: praying WITH God, declaring His promises and interceding for what is on His heart. Supplication is a personal request, asking of a special favor in a needed situation or for a special necessity, a cry for mercy or to entreat or a petition. It is a personal need or for a group, when intercession is for others, for promises or for long-term revival in an area, such as the marketplace. Some characteristics of Supplication prayer are that it is: personal, specific, according to God's word and with His timing.

Key scriptures for Supplication
- Daniel 10:11-12- from the first day that you set your heart ...your words were heard."
- Matthew 21:22- "And whatever things you ask in prayer, believing, you will receive."

FREQUENTLY USED **HARTLEY INSTITUTE TERMS**

THE ROYAL JOURNEY OF HOPE

<u>THE HOPE ROOM</u>: like the Upper Room of Acts, the Hope Room is the place we get our eyes above the clouds of doubt and despair and we focus on who God is. In the Hope Room we experience the "Good God" and begin to delight in Him all of life.
- Proverbs 16:15- "In the light of the king's countenance is life; And his favor is as a cloud of the latter rain."

<u>THE GOD OF LIFE ROOM</u>: the place where we gain the understanding that God is sovereign over every part of life, and He also really enjoys and delights in every arena, and all 7 mountains of influence and His nature is to be discovered there! We can partner with Him in government, education, business, family, the church, media, and arts and entertainment! Our unique worship is unlocked in this place.
- Psalm 119:54- "your statutes have been my songs in the house of my pilgrimage."
- Psalm 84

<u>THE COUNSEL TABLE ROOM</u>: the place that the Lord invites us into, a place of communion and intimacy at His Counsel table, where we enter into "asking" which is the second reality of Psalm 27:4 – "*to inquire in His temple.*" We ask God questions according to His hope-filled loving nature, and He gives us the right questions.
<u>Here are some questions to ask Him</u>:
- What is one thing about Your nature that I really understand?
- What are your plans to prosper this person's life?
- What is your 3-5 year plan to build this city after Your kingdom?
- What does prayer mean to You?

<u>THE PROCLAMATION ROOM:</u> the place where we have confidence in what we have heard at the Counsel Table from the Father's voice and we proclaim a thing and it happens. We partner with what is on the Father's heart and declare it into the earth.
- Isaiah 45:11- "...concerning the work of my hands command ye me."

FREQUENTLY USED **HARTLEY INSTITUTE TERMS**

GENERAL TERMS

ADORATION PILLARS: Psalm 40 special friends of Jesus, who are totally fixed in love for the son of God and are filled with hope and are confident in Him. They have seen Him in all of life and they are adorers! They are empowered with His presence in all of life and they carry His fragrance and presence wherever they go!
- Psalm 40:3- "He put a new song in my mouth, a hymn of praise to our God. Many will see and fear and put their trust in the LORD."

CHAMBER DOORS: an opening up of the knowledge of God in specific ways as in Song of Solomon 1:3 and Revelation 4:1.
- Revelation 4:1- "After this I looked, .. a door standing open in heaven."

HOPE SONGS: songs that move us from love that secures our heart into an understanding of the nature of the God of the Day and the God of Life that advances our hearts in hope
- Psalm 149:5- "Let the saints exult in glory: Let them sing for joy upon their beds."

THOSE WHO SING THE SONG OF WISDOM AND HOPE: those who hear the voice of the Father, and speak His wisdom and plans (rather than the worlds or their own) into their cities and nations on all levels.

HOPE TOOLS FOR YOUR JOURNEY

Hope Kit- $85

This Hope Kit includes the best Hope feedings to launch you into your journey of hope! A $145 value! This kit includes:
- The Hope DVD Series
- New Adoration Prayer Book
- The Journey of Hope Book
- Four Prayer CD's (Face of God as Redeemer, Supplier, Builder and the Wise God)

Adoration Prayer Booklet $15.00 (2 for $25, 3 for $30)

The Adoration Prayer Booklet is a foundational advanced tool that helps you to develop your own love language with the King of Kings, guiding you into deep adoration and intimacy with our beautiful God through devotional prayer. This book is an exploration of the attributes and character of our Great God,, arranged by the letters of the alphabet, with scriptural references and sections for journaling and adding in your own examples and heartfelt language. Great for children and families too!

52 Weeks of Hope- $25 per month

Next on the Journey, get connected each week, as Bob Hartley has recorded special "fireside chats" where he shares the most important keys for living an abundant life in God with a living hope for today! This weekly 10 minute video clip is sent directly to your email, and includes practical building blocks to apply to your week, as you embark on this journey of hope! Sign up at 52weeksofhope.com

Centcom Broadcast every Tuesday night- **FREE

Don't miss our weekly "Hope Broadcast" on Centcom.tv that gives great practical building blocks and insight into the heart of God for the present hour in the Body of Christ. Broadcast every Tuesday night at 7pm, and archived for the remainder of the week, is a fresh prophetic teaching on how to live as a Hope Reformer and impact your family, business, city and nation with the life-changing force of Hope in

HOPE IS...

An Anticipation and Belief
in God for Good in All of Life

A LIFESTYLE

the Substance of Faith

A PERSPECTIVE OF ABUNDANT LIFE

a chosen desire -

an expectation of fulfillment

an unseen invisible power

Solution Oriented

Love SECURES the heart,
but hope ADVANCES the heart

HOPE ENABLES US TO SEE
A VERY, VERY, VERY LONG WAY OUT

Made in the USA
Charleston, SC
23 January 2011